Wilderness Survival Skills

Karl McCullough

Wilderness Survival Skills
by Karl McCullough

ISBN 978-1-926917-12-2

Printed in the United States of America

TABLE OF CONTENTS

Introduction to
Survival Skills

Introduction

Surviving a dangerous situation is often more about understanding a few basics about surviving in the wilderness or in other dangerous situations. There are many principles that should be understood in order to increase your chances of survival, including how to obtain water, procure food, light a fire and build a shelter.

In this guide we are going to explore the basics, including how to build a survival kit that is well stocked should you ever find yourself in any type of situation in which your survival depends upon it.

Ready to learn how to survive in a dangerous situation?

Let's get started!

Chapter 1

Getting Started

Survival Skills Basics

Your best hope for surviving a dangerous situation is ensuring you are prepared and knowledgeable regarding certain survival skill basics. In this section we are going to explore several of the basics that are imperative to surviving any dangerous situation.

Size up the Situation

Whenever you are in a dangerous situation, it is imperative to first keep your wits about you and size up the situation. Security is always priority in this type of situation. Make use of your senses of smell, sight and hearing to get a feel for your surroundings. All of this will help you to make a survival plan.

Size up your Surroundings

Take a few moments to determine the pattern for your surroundings and what is taking place around you. Every environment in the world, regardless of whether it is desert, jungle or forest has a pattern or a rhythm. This pattern may include bird or animal noises or the sounds of insects. Understanding this pattern can help you to determine what is normal for that environment and what is not so that you will have a better sense of approaching danger.

Size up your Own Physical Condition

Once you have made note of your surroundings it is time to take note of your own physical condition. When you are in a survival situation you must carefully note any wounds you may have and apply first aid while also taking care to prevent any further injury or harm. You will need to ensure you are drinking plenty of fluids to prevent dehydration from occurring. If you are in a climate that is cold or wet, you will need to use additional clothing to prevent hypothermia from occurring.

Size up your Tools and Equipment

The next important step is to survey your tools and equipment. Check to determine what is available to you and also its condition. Now that you have taken stock of your situation as well as your surroundings, equipment and physical condition the next step is to begin creating a survival plan. This plan will focus on the basic needs for survival; food, water and shelter.

Utilize All of your Senses

When you are in a survival situation the wrong move can result in possible danger or even death. This is why it is imperative that you make full use of all of your senses before you make any move or decision. Acting in haste can be dangerous. Plan each move that you make. Ensure you are ready to move quickly but without endangering yourself. Use all of your senses to evaluate every situation by noting smells and sounds and being sensitive to changes in temperatures. You must always be observant.

Recall Where you Are

Make a point to note your location on a map if one is available to you and relate it to the terrain that is surrounding you. This is a very basic principle but it is one that is extremely important. If you are with others, always make sure you know their location as well. Pay extremely close attention to your location and the direction you are moving. Never simply rely on others in your group to track your route. Continually orient yourself to your location and make sure you know how your location is relevant to the location of water sources and areas that will provide concealment and shelter.

Vanquish Panic and Fear

Fear and panic can be your enemies in a survival situation. If you do not control these emotions it can be difficult to make a decision that is based on sound intelligence. Fear and panic can cause you to make decisions based on your feelings instead of the actual situation. They can also drain you of energy.

Improvise

In most modern societies, we do not have to worry about finding the items required for basic survival. In a dangerous situation, that is not always the case. You must be able to improvise and take tools and equipment that were originally designed for one purpose and utilize them for other uses. Natural resources can also often be used for a variety of different needs. For instance, a rock can be utilized for a hammer.

Value Surviving

Every single person has a natural instinct to live but many of us are accustomed to a life of comfort. Discomfort and inconvenience are uncomfortable and unpleasant. When faced with a dangerous situation it is imperative to place the value for surviving above the value for comfort and convenience.

Adapt to your Environment

One element that the natives of many of the most remote areas of the world share in common is that they have adapted to their environment. The same is also true of animals. In order to survive a dangerous situation, you must learn to do the same. Maintain a constant vigil and observe how the local animals behave in the environment, where they go for food and water, when they sleep, when they rise, etc. While not all of the local foods that are consumed by animals are safe for human consumption, this type of observance can give you important clues to how to survive in that environment.

Learn Basic Skills

Living by your wits and being willing to learn basic skills are essential to surviving a dangerous situation. Basic survival skills are imperative. The time to learn these skills is now, not when you are faced with a survival situation. Furthermore, it is important to take the time to practice those skills to reduce fear of the unknown and obtain the self-confidence that is necessary to actually live by your wits.

Understanding your Natural Reactions

It is also important to understand the natural reactions you are likely to encounter when faced with a survival situation. Your ability to adapt both mentally and physically to a challenging situation is crucial to survival.

Fear

Fear is a natural emotional response to any dangerous situation. You may be surprised to discover that much like stress, fear can actually have a positive impact when it encourages caution rather than recklessness. Fear can also be dangerous as it can immobilize you and prevent you from taking actions that are necessary for survival. Most people will experience some degree of fear when faced with unfamiliar surroundings and dangerous conditions. There is no reason to be ashamed of this but it is important to be able to overcome your fears.

Anxiety

Anxiety is commonly associated with fear. It is completely natural to experience fear as well as anxiety. Anxiety is that sense of apprehension or unease you feel when you are faced with a situation that is dangerous. Anxiety can also be used in a healthy way to encourage you to take action. Like fear, it is also important to learn to manage your anxiety so that it does not overwhelm you to the point that you experience difficulty in thinking, making decisions or taking action.

Frustration and Anger

When you are not able to reach your goals you may experience frustration and/or anger. The sole goal of survival is to remain alive until you can reach assistance. Often minimal resources are available to you in this type of situation, which means that eventually you will experience frustration or anger as you must cope with damaged equipment, becoming lost, the weather or any other assortment of problems. When you are frustrated or anger you may give in to irrational behavior, impulsive reactions, decisions that are not well thought out, etc. When frustration and anger are properly harnessed they can help you to meet the challenges you may face.

Depression

Another common emotion that may be experienced in a survival situation is depression. This can commonly stem from anger and frustration. The main problem with depression is that you may begin to give up and give in to feelings of helplessness and hopelessness. It is imperative that you do not give in to such feelings as they can drain your will to survive.

Boredom and Loneliness

By nature, most people are social and need the company of other people to feel complete, at least some of the time. When you are isolated in a dangerous situation, loneliness and boredom can lead to depression. It is crucial that you find ways to keep occupied to prevent this from happening.

Chapter 2
Survival Planning

Survival Kits

Survival planning is dependent upon the recognition that at some point you could face a dangerous situation and taking the necessary steps to improve your chances of survival. Therefore, survival planning is really just a matter of preparation. Preparation involves ensuring you have necessary survival items and also that you are knowledgeable about how to use those items.

The Importance of Planning

There are many important aspects of survival planning, including understanding how to use preventive medicine and preparing and having a survival kit with you. Most aviators ensure they have a survival kit onboard for the type of environment they will be flying over. Even if you are not an aviator, it is important to have a survival kit to give you the best chances of survival should you find yourself in a dangerous situation. Even a relatively small survival kit can prove to be life-saving when you are facing a dangerous situation.

Survival Kits

The type of environment in which you may find yourself will determine the types of items that should be included in your survival kit. The amount of equipment included in your survival kit will be based on the way you plan to carry your kit. If you plan to carry your kit on your body you will naturally need a smaller kit than would be needed if you are able to carry it in a vehicle.

Layering your survival kit is imperative. The most important items should always be kept on your body, such as your compass and your map. Lesser important items should be kept with load-bearing equipment.

While preparing your survival kit, take care to choose items that will serve more than one purpose. For instance, if you have two items that can serve the same purpose, choose one that can also serve another function. Items should not be duplicated as this will only increase the weight and size of your kit.

Keep in mind that you do not necessarily need an elaborate survival kit. Only functional items should be included along with a case for holding those items. You should ensure the case meets the following qualifications:

- Waterproof or water repellant
- Easy to carry or can be attached to the body
- Durable

Within your survival kit you should include the following items:

- First aid items
- Fire starting equipment
- Water purification drops or tablets
- Shelter items
- Food procurement items
- Signaling items

Good examples of these items include:
- Wrist compass
- Candle
- Fishhooks
- Lighter, waterproof matches, metal match
- Snare wire

- Small hand lens
- Water purification tablets
- Surgical blades
- Solar blanket
- Lip balm
- Knife
- Butterfly sutures

Basic Survival Medicine

Medical problems can compromise your ability to achieve a return to safety and compromise your situation. A lack of both medical supplies and training can make it difficult to treat illness and injury. The ability to treat yourself and others will help to alleviate feelings of helplessness and give you a sense of self-confidence that can be extremely important to your ultimate survival.

Basic Requirements to Maintain Health

In order to survive any situation you must have food and water. You must also be able to observe basic personal hygiene.

Water

The human body loses a great deal of water through normal body processes such as urinating and sweating. The average adult will lose between two and three liters of water per day. Other factors, including exposure to cold, heat exposure, high altitude, intense activity, illness or burns can result in the loss of more water. To survive, you must replace this water.

Dehydration occurs as a result of not adequately replacing body fluids as they are lost. Dehydration can decrease your efficiency and also increase your susceptibility to further injury or severe shock. The results of dehydration include:

5% Loss of Body Fluids-thirst, nausea, irritability, weakness

10% Loss of Body Fluids-headache, dizziness, tingling in the limbs and inability to walk

15% Loss of Body Fluids-painful urination, dim vision, deafness, swollen tongue, numbness of the skin

More than 15% Loss of Body Fluids-Possible death

Symptoms of Dehydration
- Low urine output
- Dark urine that has a strong odor
- Fatigue
- Dark, sunken eyes
- Emotional instability
- Delayed capillary refill in the beds of the fingernails

- Loss of skin elasticity
- Trench line in the center of the tongue
- Thirst

It is important to keep in mind that by the time you crave fluids you are already 2% dehydrated.

Water must be replaced as it is lost. In a survival situation it can be difficult to make up for this deficit. Do not rely on your thirst as an indication of how much water your body requires. As a general rule, most people are not able to drink more than one liter of water at a time comfortably. Therefore, even when you are not actually thirsty it is important to drink small amounts of waters on a regular basis in order to prevent dehydration from occurring.

You should also increase your water intake when you are under mental or physical stress or you are in extreme conditions. Make sure you drink a sufficient amount of liquids to maintain urine output of 0.5 liters every 24 hours.

When you are in a situation where you are not able to consume more than a small amount of food you should make sure you are drinking between 6 and 8 liters of water per day. When you are in arid conditions you could easily lose as much as 3.5 liters of water per hour. In this type of situation you need to drink up to 30 liters of water per day.

As your body loses water, you also lose body salts or electrolytes. In most circumstances, your diet can help to make up for these losses but when you are faced with illness or an extreme situation your body will need additional sources of electrolytes. Mixing ¼ teaspoon salt to one liter of water will provide the concentrated electrolytes your body needs.

In a survival situation numerous physical problems can be encountered. Of all of those problems, dehydration is the most preventable. The following guidelines can help you to avoid dehydration:

- When eating, always drink water. Water is used as part of the digestive process and can result in dehydration.

- Limit sweat producing activities

- Ration water using common sense. Consuming 0.5 liter of a mixture of 2 teaspoons sugar to one liter of water will help to prevent severe dehydration for at least one week as long as you are limiting activity and heat loss or gain.

Fluid loss can be estimated through a variety of methods. For instance when you have lost ¾ liter of water the pulse rate for your wrist will be less than 100 beats per minute. Your breathing rate will be between 12 and 20 beats per minute.

With a fluid loss of up to 1.5 liters the pulse rate will be between 100 and 120 beats per minute and your breath rate will be between 20 and 30 breaths per minute. At a loss of up to 2 liters, the pulse rate will reach up to 140 beats per minute and you will have a breath rate of up to 40 breaths per minute.

Food

It is possible to actually live for several weeks without any food; however, to remain healthy you do need an adequate amount of food. Both physical and mental capabilities will deteriorate at a rapid rate without food. You will also become quite weak. Food is imperative to replenishing the substances burned by the body and to also provide energy as well as minerals, vitamins, salts and other elements which are essential for maintaining optimal health.

There are two basic sources of food, which are animals and plants. Both offer varying degrees of fats, carbohydrates, proteins and calories.

Calories are a way of measuring potential energy and heat. On average, a person requires 2,000 calories per day just to function at a basic level. Without a sufficient amount of fats, carbohydrates and proteins through adequate caloric intake, you will begin to starve and the body will begin to consume its own tissues just for energy.

Plant Foods

Plant foods provide the main source of energy, which are carbohydrates. Many plants also provide a sufficient amount of protein for the body as well. Plants do not typically provide a balanced diet but can sustain you in an extreme situation. Such foods include nuts, seeds, green vegetables, roots, etc.

Animal Foods

Meat tends to be more nourishing than plant food and is also often more readily available in many areas. In order to obtain meat food you must understand the habits of various types of wildlife and how to successfully capture it. In a survival situation it is important to first seek out the wildlife that is most abundant and most easily obtained. This may include fish, reptiles, crustaceans and insects. These types of foods can satisfy your hunger while you prepare snares and traps for obtaining larger game.

Personal Hygiene

Cleanliness is imperative in any situation for preventing disease and infection. The simple fact is that poor hygiene can decrease your chances of survival.

While it would be nice to be able to have a shower each day, this is a luxury in a survival situation. A cloth and soapy water may be the best you are able to do in this type of situation. Make sure you pay careful attention to the armpits, feet, hands and genitals as these areas are the most vulnerable for infection and infestation.

It is particularly important to make sure the hair and hands are kept clean. When you have germs on the hands, it can result in infection of wounds and food. Always wash your hands any time you handle materials that are likely to carry germs as well as after caring for anyone that is sick and relieving yourself. Make a point to keep the fingernails clean and trimmed. The hair should also be kept clean to prevent the infestation of lice, fleas and other parasites.

In addition, you should keep your clothing as well as your bedding clean to reduce the risk of infection and infestation. Whenever your clothing becomes soiled make sure you clean it. Try to wear clean socks and underclothing each day. If water is limited, air your clothing out in the sun for at least two hours.

Caring for your Teeth

Make a point to clean your teeth and mouth at least once per day. If you do not have a toothbrush available, use a chewing stick. A chewing stick can be made from a twig that is several inches in length. Chew on one end of the stick to separate the different fibers. It can then be used for brushing the teeth.

Caring for your Feet

In order to prevent serious problems with the feet make sure you wash the feet daily. Keep the toenails trimmed straight across. Check the feet daily for blisters. If you should happen to get a blister, do not try to open it. Blisters that are intact are better protected from becoming infected. Try using a padding material around the blister to reduce friction and pressure.

Chapter 3

Shelters

Types of Shelters

A shelter is imperative to provide you with protection against wind, snow, rain, insects, sun, cold or hot temperatures. In addition, a shelter can also provide you with an important sense of well-being. Your shelter must be large enough to provide adequate protection but small enough to ensure you are able to contain body heat, particularly in cold climates.

Selecting a Shelter Site

When you find yourself in a dangerous situation, selecting a shelter becomes a high priority. Therefore it is important to begin looking for a shelter as quickly as possible. Keep the following requirements in mind when choosing a shelter:

- Site must have the materials necessary for forming the type of shelter needed

- Site must be level and large enough for you to be able to lie down and be comfortable.

- Provides concealment

- Is suitable for signaling

- Provides protection from wild animals

- Is free from reptiles, insects and poisonous plants

You should also select your site in order to avoid potential problems, including the following

- Flash flood areas in foothills
- Rockslides or avalanches in mountainous terrain
- Sites near bodies of water that are beneath a high water mark

Types of Shelters

When selecting a shelter site, there are several factors that must be taken into consideration, including:

- How much effort and time will be required to construct the shelter
- Whether the shelter will provide adequate protection from the elements
- If you have the necessary tools for building that shelter or whether you can improvise tools
- If you have the right amount and type of materials required to construct the shelter

Different Types of Shelters

Poncho Lean-To

This is one of the easiest types of shelters to construct because it only takes minimal equipment and time to construct. You will need the following:

- Poncho
- 2 to 3 meters of rope
- 3 stakes
- 2 poles or 2 trees located two to three meters apart

To Construct a Poncho Lean-To

1. Tie off the hood of the poncho. Pull the drawstring tightly and then roll the hood in a long direction. Fold it into thirds and then tie it off using the drawstring.

2. Cut the rope in half. Tie half of the rope to the corner grommet on one of the long sides of the poncho. Tie the other half of the rope to the remaining corner grommet.

3. Tie a stick to each rope just beneath the grommet.

4. Tie the ropes to the trees at about waist height.

5. Spread the poncho and then anchor it into the ground by placing the sticks through the grommets and into the ground.

Poncho Tent

You can also construct a tent using a poncho. This is will help to provide protection from the elements on two sides. You will need the following:

- Poncho
- 2 1.5 meter ropes
- 6 sharpened sticks about 30 cm in length
- 2 trees about 2 to 3 meters apart

To Construct a Poncho Tent

1. Tie off the poncho hood in the same manner as when constructing the lean-to

2. Tie one of the ropes to the center grommet on either side of the poncho.

3. Tie the remaining ends of the ropes to two trees at about knee height. Stretch the poncho tightly.

4. Draw one side of the poncho tightly and then anchor it to the ground using sharpened sticks to push through the grommets. Do the same on the other side.

3 Hole Parachute Tepee

If you have a parachute available along with three poles, you can make a tepee. This type of shelter is very easy to construct and does not take much time. It will also provide you with protection from the elements and provide you with space for signaling while also providing sufficient space for more than one person as well as equipment. A tepee can also allow space for cooking, storing firewood and sleeping.

To Construct a Parachute Tepee

1. Position the poles on the ground and tie them together at one end.
2. Stand the frame upright and position the poles to form a tripod.
3. Place additional poles against the tripod for more support. 6 poles are ideal. They should not be tied to the tripod.
4. Locate the entrance at least 90 degrees from the direction of the wind.
5. Position the parachute on the back of the tripod.
6. Position the loop of the bridle over the top of the canopy of the teepee.
7. Wrap the canopy around one side of the

tripod.

8. Wrap the folded edges of the canopy around two of the free standing poles to build the entrance.

9. Position the additional canopy beneath the poles of the tepee to create a floor.

10. Allow a 30 to 50 centimeter opening at the top of the tepee for ventilation if you plan to have a fire inside.

Field Lean-To

If you are in a forest or wooded area and there are sufficient natural materials available you can make a field lean-to for shelter. You will need the following:

- Two trees about 2 meters apart
- One pole approximately 2 meters in length
- 5 to 8 poles about 3 meters in length for beams
- Vines or cord
- Additional saplings, poles or vines

To Construct a Field Lean-To

1. Tie the 2 meter pole to the trees at waist height. This will form the horizontal support.
2. Place one end of the 3 meter pole, the beam, to one side of the horizontal support. The backside of the lean-to should be positioned into the wind.
3. Take the vines or saplings and crisscross them over the beams.
4. Cover the framework of the lean-to using pine needles, leaves, grass or brush. Make sure you begin at the bottom and work your way up toward the top.
5. Use pine needles, leaves, straw or grass inside the shelter to create bedding.

Creating a Natural Shelter

Natural formations can also provide a shelter as well. Good examples include rocky crevices, caves, large rocks on the sides of hills, clumps of bushes, large trees and fallen trees. Keep the following in mind when choosing a natural shelter:

- Keep away from low ground areas such as narrow valleys, ravines or creek beds.
- Be sure to check for ticks, poisonous snakes, scorpions, mites and stinging ants
- Be on the lookout for dead limbs, loose rocks or any other natural growth that could fall

Debris Hut

This type of shelter is excellent for providing ease of construction and warmth. To create a debris hut:

- Construct a tripod using two short stakes along with a long ridgepole.
- Secure the ridgepole by anchoring it to the tree at waist height.
- Prop large sticks on both sides of the ridgepole.
- Place thinner sticks and brush in a cross-wise manner on the framework.
- Pile insulating material near the entrance that can be dragged inside to create a door or close the entrance to your shelter

Beach Shade Shelter

A beach shade shelter will provide protection from wind, rain, sun and heat. It is also easy to create using natural materials that may be available to you in a beach setting. To construct a beach shade shelter:

- Collect driftwood or other natural materials that can be used as support beams
- Choose a site for your shelter that is above the high water mark
- Dig out a trench that runs north to south. The trench should be wide enough and long enough to lie down comfortably.
- Pile up sand on three sides of the trench.
- Position support beams across the trench on top of the mound. This will form a framework for the roof.
- You can dig out more sand in front of the entrance to make it larger.
- Utilize natural materials like leaves or grass to construct a bed inside the shelter.

Desert Shelter

When you are in an arid environment it is important to consider the effort, time and materials that are necessary for forming a shelter. Provided that you have materials such as a canvas, parachute or poncho you can use it with features in the natural terrain such as mounds of sand, a rock outcropping or a depression with the rocks or dune to construct a shelter.

For Rock Outcroppings

- Anchor one end of the canvas or poncho or other material along one edge of the rock outcropping
- Extend and then anchor the remaining end of the material to provide the best shade.

In Sandy Areas

- Construct a mound of sand or use the side of a sand dune to create one side of the shelter
- Anchor one end of the material along the top of the mound. Use sand or other weights that may be available
- Extend and then anchor the remaining end of the material to provide the best shade

Chapter 4

Water Procurement

Water Sources

Water is one of the most important needs when in a survival situation. It is simply not possible to survive long without water, particularly when you are in an arid or hot area where you will be losing water rapidly through perspiration. Even when you are in a cold area, you will still require a minimum of two liters of water per day.

There is water to some degree in practically any environment.

Frigid Area-In a frigid area you can use ice and snow as a water source, provided that you melt and purify if first. Remember that ice and snow are not any more pure than the environment from which they come.

Sea-When in a sea environment you can use sea water provided that it is desalted first. Never drink sea water unless it has been desalted using a desalting kit. You can also collect rain water using a container or tarp.

Beach environment-You may be able to obtain water from the ground in a beach environment by digging a hole deep enough to allow the water to seep inside.

Desert environment-When in a dessert environment you may also be able to collect water by digging a deep hole.

At times water can be collected from crevices in rocks or trees. Try using a cloth to stuff inside the crevice to absorb the water and then wring it from the cloth. Remember to always purify water before drinking it.

In some cases you may be able to obtain water from tropical vines. Cut a notch in the vine as high as you are able to reach and then cut the vine off near the ground. You can catch the liquid as it drops either in your mouth or in a container. Do not drink any liquid that is milky, bitter tasting or sticky.

The milk that is present in unripe coconuts can quench your thirst but make sure you drink milk from mature coconuts only in moderation as it acts as a laxative. The roots of plants can also provide water. Try digging the roots from the ground and then cut them into short pieces and smash the pulp until the moisture runs out. You can then catch the liquid using a container. Some stalks, stems and leaves also contain water. Notch or cut the stalks near the base of a joint to drain the liquid. Trees which provide water include the following:

- Palms-palm trees such as the coconut, buri, rattan and sugar contain liquid.
- Traveler's tree-this tree is found in Madagascar
- Umbrella tree-the roots and leaf bases of the tree can provide water. It is found in western tropical Africa.
- Baobab tree-this tree is found in northern Australia and Africa and collects water in the trunk during the wet season.

Keep in mind that sap from plants should not be kept for longer than 24 hours or it will begin to ferment and can become dangerous.

How to Purify Water

Rainwater that is collected in a clean container or a plant is typically safe for drinking purposes. Water from ponds, lakes, springs, swamps or streams should be purified, especially if located in the tropics or near human settlements.

Water can be purified using chlorine or iodine or by boiling. You can also use water purification tablets. Place 5 drops of iodine in a canteen full of clear water. If the water is at all cloudy, use 10 drops. Allow the water to stand for at least 30 minutes prior to drinking. You can also purify water by boiling it for one minute at sea level.

Add one minute for each additional 300 meters that you are above sea level. Or, you can boil water for 10 minutes regardless of your location to be safe.

Keep in mind that when you drink nonpotable water you can swallow dangerous organisms or contract diseases, including:

- Dysentery-prolonged, severe diarrhea
- Typhoid and cholera
- Flukes-if you swallow flukes they can bore into your bloodstream and cause disease
- Leeches-if you swallow leeches it can create a bleeding wound that can become infected

Chapter 5

Building a Fire

Basic Principles of Building a Fire

The ability to start a fire is extremely important when faced with a survival situation and can even make the difference between surviving and not surviving. Fire is crucial for many purposes. Not only can it help in the preservation and cooking of food but it can also provide comfort and warmth. Water can also be used to sterilize bandages, purify water, signal for help and provide protection from wild animals. It is also important to understand the fire can result in problems as well, including possible forest fires or carbon monoxide poisoning when used inside a shelter.

In order to build a fire, it is important to understand the basic principles of fire. Fuel, when in a nongaseous state, will not burn directly. When heat is applied to a fuel, gas is produced. When this gas is combined with oxygen within the air it will burn.

To correctly construct and maintain a fire it is important to understand the concept behind the fire triangle. The three sides of the fire triangle are represented by heat, air and fuel. The removal of any of these elements will cause a fire to go out. The correct ratio of all of these elements is important to allow a fire to burn at maximum capability. Practice is extremely important in being able to build a fire using these elements.

Site Selection and Preparation for Building a Fire

Prior to building a fire you will need to locate a site and make arrangements. Consider the following:

- The climate and terrain in which you are located
- The tools and materials available
- How much time is available
- Why a fire is needed
- Security of the area

Begin by looking for a dry spot that has the following elements:

- Protection from the wind
- Suitably located to your shelter
- Able to concentrate heat in the desired direction
- An available supply of wood or fuel

If you are in an area that is covered with brush or wooded, you can clear the brush and then scrape the surface oil from the area selected. Make sure you clear an area that is a minimum of 1 meter in diameter to prevent the fire from spreading. If you have a sufficient amount of time you can build a fire wall using rocks or logs. This will assist in directing the heat in the desired direction while also reducing flying sparks and the chance of the fire spreading. Make sure you do not use porous or wet rocks as they could explode when heated.

Building an Underground Fireplace

In some cases, you might be able to build an underground fireplace. This will conceal the fire and allow you to cook food. To build an underground fireplace:

- Dig a hole in the ground
- Dig a large connecting hole to allow for ventilation on the upwind side of the first hole
- Build a fire in the hole

Selecting Fire Material

You will need three types of material to build a fire; kindling, tinder and fuel. Tinder is a type of dry material that will ignite without a lot of heat. All it takes is a spark to start a fire. Tinder must be completely dry to ensure the spark will ignite the tinder. Charred cloth works well, especially if you only have a device for generating sparks. You can create charred cloth by heating cotton cloth until it has turned black but has not burned.

It will need to be kept airtight to remain dry. You should prepare this type of cloth in advance and keep it in your survival kit.

Kindling is any type of combustible material that can be added to burning tinder. This material must be completely dry to ensure it will burn rapidly. Kindling will increase the temperature of the fire.

Fuel is less combustible and will burn slowly and steadily once it has been ignited.

Tinder
- Birch bark
- Shredded inner bark from chestnut, cedar or red elm trees
- Fine wood shavings
- Dead ferns, moss or grass
- Straw
- Sawdust
- Dead evergreen needles
- Fine, dried vegetable fibers
- Dead palm leaves
- Gunpowder
- Cotton
- Lint

Kindling

- Split wood
- Small strips of wood
- Small twigs
- Heavy cardboard

Dry branches or standing wood Fuel

- Dry inside of braches or fallen wood
- Green wood that is finely split
- Dry grasses split into bunches
- Dried animal dung
- Animal fats
- Coal or oil lying near the surface

Steps for Building a Fire

There are many different methods that can be used for laying a fire.

Tepee Method

To make a fire using this method you will need to arrange the tinder along with a few sticks of kindling in the shape of a cone or tepee. Light the center. The outside logs will fall inward as the tepee burns, which will feed the fire. This method is good for using with wet wood.

Lean-to Method

To make a fire using this method, push a green stick into the ground at a 30 degree angle. Point the end of the stick in the same direction of the wind. Place tinder deep within the lean-to stick. Position pieces of kindling against the stick. Light the tinder. You will need to add more kindling as the kindling catches fire from the tinder.

Cross-Ditch

To make a fire using this method, scratch a cross in the ground. The cross should be about 30 centimeters in size. Dig the cross at least 7 centimeters deep. Place a wad of tinder in the middle of the cross. Building a pyramid of kindling above the tinder. The shallow ditch will allow air to sweep beneath the tinder to provide an essential draft for the fire.

Pyramid

To make a fire using this method, position to small branches or logs parallel on the ground. Next, place a layer of small logs solidly across the logs. Add three or four more branches or logs. Each layer should be smaller than the one below it. Make a starter fire directly on top of the pyramid. The starter fire will ignite the logs below as the fire burns. This will provide you with a fire that will burn downward and will not require any attention throughout the night.

Lighting a Fire

There are also many ways in which you can ef-fectively lay a fire. The material available within the area and your particular situation will dictate which method is most suitable. Remember to always light the fire from the upwind side. The tinder, kindling and fuel should be laid so that the fire will burn as long as needed. There are two categories of igniters that can be used to pro-vide the initial heat to start tinder burning. These methods include primitive and modern methods.

Modern Ignition Methods

Matches-matches should always be kept water-proof. Convex lens-this method can be used on a bright, sunny day. The lens can be taken from a camera, binocular or magnifying glass. Angle the lens so that the sun's rays are concentrated on the tinder. Hold the lens over the same spot until the tinder has begun to smolder. Gently fan or blow the tinder into a flame and then apply it to the fire lay.

Metal match-you can use a flat, dry leaf beneath the tinder with a small part exposed. Take the tip of the metal match and place it on the leaf, hold-ing the match in one hand and a knife in the other hand. Scrape the knife against the metal match to create sparks. The sparks should hit the tinder and cause it to smolder. Battery-you can also use a battery to create a spark. This method is actually dependent upon the type of battery that is available to you. Attach a wire to each terminal of the battery. Touch the ends of the wires together near the tinder. The sparks should ignite the tinder.

Gunpowder-if you have ammunition available you can carefully extract the bullet from the shell casing and then use the gunpowder for tinder. A spark is all that is needed to ignite the powder, so you must be extremely careful as you extract the bullet from the casing.

Primitive Methods

Flint and steel-the easiest of all the primitive methods for lighting a fire is the direct spark method. You can strike a flint or any other type of rock edge with a hard sharp edge using a piece of carbon steel. Keep in mind that stainless steel will not usually produce as effective of a spark. This method does require some practice. Once the spark has caught the tinder, blow on it to cause the spark to spread and create flames.

Tips for Building a Fire

- Collect tinder and kindling along the trail
- Keep firewood dry
- Add insect repellent to tinder
- Bank fires to keep coals alive throughout the night
- Dry damp firewood near the fire
- When possible, use non-aromatic seasoned hardwood for fuel
- Always make sure the fire it out prior to leaving camp
- Do choose wood lying on the ground even if it appears to be dry

Chapter 6

Procuring Food

Animals for Food

After water, your most urgent need in a survival situation is food. It is imperative to keep in mind that your three most important needs in a surival situation are water, food and shelter.

In most cases you should concentrate your efforts on smaller animals rather than larger game. Smaller game tends to be more abundant and also easier to obtain as well as prepare. In procuring food it is important to spend time learning the habits as well as the behavioral patterns of different animals. You can safely eat almost anything that swims, walks, crawls or flies with very few exceptions. Remember that although it may seem distasteful, in order to survive you must eat what is available to you.

Insects

The most abundant life form comes in the form of insects. They are easily caught and can provide as much as 80% protein compared to the 20% that comes from beef. Although they might not be overly appetizing, insects can prove to be a good food source. Of course, you should avoid any insects that bite or sting as well as any brightly colored or hairy insects. You should also avoid insects that have any heavy odor. Furthermore, avoid spiders and any insects that commonly carry diseases such as mosquitoes, flies and ticks.

One of the best places to look for a variety of different insects can be found in rotting logs on the ground. Here you can find beetles, ants, termites and grubs. Insect nests may also be found directly on the ground including on grassy areas in fields. Look around boards, stones and any other materials that may be lying on the ground as well. Keep in mind that insect larvae can also be eaten. Grasshoppers and beetles will have a hard outer shell that may have parasites. They should be cooked prior to eating. Barbed legs and winds should be removed. Most insects can be eaten raw. You may be surprised to find that some insects actually have a sweet taste because they store honey in their bodies.

Worms

Worms are also a good source of protein. You can dig for them in damp soil or keep an eye out for them following a rain shower. Keep in mind that worms should be washed in clean, potable water after they are captured. The worm will naturally purge and then you can eat it raw.

Crustaceans

Freshwater shrimp can reach up to 2.5 centimeters and can be found in lakes or ponds. Crayfish are much like crabs or lobsters and can be distinguishes by their five pairs of legs and their hard exoskeleton. Crayfish tend to be active at night but can also be located during the daytime by looking near stones in streams. They also tend to bury into soft mud.

Mollusks

This class includes saltwater and freshwater shellfish such as clams, snails, mussels, barnacles, sea urchins and periwinkles. Look in wet sand and tidal pools. You may also have look near rocks along beaches. Keep in mind that mussels can be poisonous in tropical zones during the summer months. Mollusks should be baked, boiled or steamed in the shell. Never eat shellfish that have not been covered by water at high tide.

Fish

Fish also provide a good source of fat and protein. They are usually quite abundant. To have the most success at catching fish, it is important to understand their habits. For instance, fish tend to feed right before a storm and will not feed when water is swollen and muddy. Light can attract fish at night. Fish often gather in areas where there are deep pools, overhanging brush and near logs or other objects that can provide shelter.

You do not have to worry about poisonous freshwater fish. Catfish do have protrusions on their dorsal fins and barbs that are sharp and needle-like and which can inflict very painful wounds that may become infected.

All freshwater fish should be cooked to kill parasites before consuming. Saltwater fish should be cooked as a precaution as well. Marine life that is obtained farther out to sea typically does not contain parasites and can be eaten raw. There are some species of saltwater fish that may have flesh that is poisonous. Examples include triggerfish, porcupine fish, cowfish, oilfish, thorn fish, puffer, jack and red snapper.

Amphibians

Salamanders and frogs can usually be found fairly easily in bodies of fresh water. Frogs tend to bury themselves in debris and mud. Keep in mind that there are actually some poisonous species of frogs. You should avoid any frogs that have an X on their back or are brightly colored.

Toads should not be confused with frogs. Toads are usually found in dry environments. Toads can also be poisonous so they should be avoided.

Salamanders tend to be nocturnal and therefore the best time to catch them is at night and with a light. Look around rocks in water or in mud banks.

Reptiles

Reptiles are also a good source of protein and can be caught rather easily. They should be cooked but can be eaten raw in an emergency. The flesh of reptiles can transmit parasites but due to the fact that reptiles are cold-blooded they do not carry blood diseases.

Birds

All species of birds can be eaten. The flavor of different birds can vary quite a bit. Flesh-eating birds can be skinned for an improvement in taste. Pigeons and many other birds can actually be caught by hand on their roosts at night. It can be much easier to catch many birds if you understand where and when they nest.

Mammals

Mammals provide an excellent source of protein and tend to be tasty. There are some disadvantages to obtaining mammals as a food source, including possible injury depending on the size of the animal. All mammals can be eaten; although it should be kept in mind that the bearded seal and polar bear actually have toxic levels of Vitamin A within their livers. The platypus, which is native to Tasmania and Australia, has poisonous glands. Some scavenging animals may potentially carry diseases.

Using Plants to Survive

There are actually many plants that can be eaten, provided that you do not choose the wrong plant. Plants can also be used as weapons and for constructing shelters and building fires. When using plants for foods it is imperative to avoid being accidentally poisoned. You should only eat those plants which can be positively identified and which you know are safe for eating.

When collecting wild plants for food, keep the following in mind:

- Plants that grow near occupied buildings and homes have likely been sprayed with pesticides and should be thoroughly washed.

- Plants that grow in contaminated water are also contaminated and must be disinfected or boiled.

- Some plants may contain fungal toxins and should be avoided if they show any signs of fungus or mildew.

- Even plants of the same species can differ in regards to toxicity.

- Some people have a higher level of sensitivity to plants than others. If you tend to be sensitive, you should avoid any unknown wild plants.

- You should never eat mushrooms when you are in a survival situation. The only foolproof way to tell if a mushroom is edible is by positive identification. When you are in a survival situation there is no room for experimenting.

Identifying Plants

Leaf shapes can be used for identifying plants along with root structure and leaf arrangements.

The basic leaf shapes are:
- egg-shaped
- elliptical
- lance-shaped
- wedge-shape
- long-pointed
- triangular
- top-shaped

Leaf margins may be:
- Smooth
- Toothless
- Lobed
- Toothed

Leaves may be arranged in
- Alternate
- Opposite
- Simple
- Compound
- basal rosette patterns

The basic types of root structures include:
- Clove
- Bulb
- Tuber
- Corm
- Rhizome
- Taproot
- Crown

Bulbs are similar to onions and will have concentric rings when sliced in half. Cloves are similar to garlic. Taproots are much like carrots. Tubes are like potatoes. Rhizomes have underground stems. Corms are similar to bulbs but are solid when they are cut. A crown is a type of root structure that is similar to asparagus.

It is important to learn as much as possible about plants that can be used for food. Remember that some plants are only edible at certain times of the year.

Using the Universal Edibility Test

There are many different types of plants that exist around the world. Tasting even a small amount of some plants can create discomfort or result in death. Therefore, it is important to learn about the edibility of foods before consuming any portion of it. The Universal Edibility Test can help with this. Follow these guidelines:

- Test only one portion of the food at a time.
- Separate the plant into basic components including leaves, stems, buds, roots and flowers.
- Smell the plant for acidic or strong odors.
- Remember that you should not eat for 8 hours prior to beginning the test.
- Before consuming any part of the plant, touch a small piece to your lips to test for burning or stinging
- If there is no reaction to the lips within 3 minutes, place a small portion on the

tongue for 15 minutes

- If there is no reaction, chew a small portion and hold it in your mouth for 15 minutes without swallowing
- If there is no reaction within 15 minutes, swallow
- Wait 8 hours. If you have any reaction, induce vomiting and drink plenty of water
- If there are no ill effects, eat ¼ cup of the same part of the plant prepared in the same manner. Wait 8 hours and if there are no ill effects; that part of the plant is considered safe to eat.

Tips and Guidelines

You can avoid potentially poisonous plants by staying away from any that:

- Have discolored or milky sap
- Bulbs, beans or seeds inside pods
- Has a soapy or bitter taste
- Has fine hairs, spines or thorns
- Grain heads with purplish, pink or black spurs
- Three-leaved growth pattern
- Almond scent in the leaves or woody parts

Temperate Zone Food Plants

- Amaranth
- Arrowroot
- Asparagus
- Beechnut
- Blackberries
- Blueberries
- Burdock
- Cattail
- Chestnut
- Chicory
- Chufa
- Dandelion
- Daylily
- Nettle
- Oaks
- Persimmon
- Plantain
- Pokeweed
- Prickly pear cactus
- Purslane
- Sassafras
- Sheep sorrel
- Strawberries
- Thistle
- Water lily and lotus

- Wild onion and garlic
- Wild rose
- Wood sorrel

Tropical Zone Food Plants
- Bamboo
- Bananas
- Breadfruit
- Cashew nut
- Coconut
- Mango
- Palms
- Papaya
- Sugarcane
- Taro

Desert Zone Food Plants
- Acacia
- Agave
- Cactus
- Date palm
- Desert amaranth

Seaweeds

Seaweed is a form of marine algae that is found near or on the ocean shores. There are also some edible freshwater varieties of seaweed. Seaweed can be a valuable source of iodine as well as other minerals and even Vitamin C. Keep in mind that eating too much seaweed can produce a laxative effect. Do not gather seaweed that has been on the sore for any length of time as it may be decayed or spoiled. Freshly harvested seaweed can be dried for use later.

Thin, tender seaweed can be dried over a fire or in the sun until it is crisp. It can then be added to broths or soups. Seaweed that is thick and leathery should be boiled to soften it. Some varieties can be eaten raw but should be tested for edibility.

- Dulse
- Green seaweed
- Irish moss
- Kelp
- Laver
- Mojaban
- Sugar wrack

Conclusion

When facing any type of survival situation it is important to have as much knowledge, resources and training at your disposal as possible. Doing so can mean the difference between life and death. While it is not possible to always predict the type of circumstances and environment you might find yourself when in a survival situation, practicing survival skills in advance can help to ensure you are prepared if you should find yourself in a survival situation.

Other books by Psylon Press:

100% Blonde Jokes
R. Cristi
ISBN 978-0-9866004-1-8

Choosing a Dog Breed Guide
Eric Nolah
ISBN 978-0-9866004-5-6

Best Pictures Of Paris
Christian Radulescu
ISBN 978-0-9866004-8-7

Best Gift Ideas For Women
Taylor Timms
ISBN 978-0-9866004-4-9

Top Bikini Pictures
Taylor Timms
ISBN 978-0-9866426-3-0

Cross Tattoos
Johnny Karp
ISBN 978-0-9866426-4-7

Metal Detecting Tips
Johnny Karp
ISBN 978-0-9866426-2-3

For more books please visit:

www.psylonpress.com